# A Primary Religious Education Course
## Book Three

### Richard Hughes

# Jerusalem

R. D. LIBRARY

Oxford University Press 1985

England

Jerusalem –
Antiquities

Oxford University Press, Walton Street, Oxford OX2 6DP

Oxford London
New York Toronto Melbourne Auckland
Kuala Lumpur Singapore Hong Kong Tokyo
Delhi Bombay Calcutta Madras Karachi
Nairobi Dar es Salaam Cape Town

and associated companies in
Beirut Berlin Ibadan Mexico City Nicosia

Oxford is a trade mark of Oxford University Press

Typeset by Tradespools Ltd., Frome, Somerset.
Printed in Hong Kong

# Contents

# Looking at history

The Brown family is visiting a famous fortress.

Look at the picture.

1. What is Mr Brown doing?
2. What is Peter doing?
3. What are the birds in the picture? (they are not crows or rooks)
4. Why will Peter not get a very good picture?

There are many clues in the picture to tell you where the Browns are. Here are some more. The building in the background is called the White Tower. The man in the strange uniform is sometimes called a Beefeater.

4

**Find out**

5. What is the fortress called?
6. Is there a legend about the birds?

Here is the fortress from the air.

Look at the picture

7. Can you draw a plan of the fortress?
8. Label the White Tower on your plan.

The White Tower was built by William the Conqueror. The work was begun in 1078 A.D.

**Find out**

9. Was William the Conqueror English?
10. What famous battle did he win?
11. How long ago did that battle take place?
12. What was William before he became King of England?

The ordinary people of England were Saxons. The rulers of England were Normans. William built the White Tower for himself and his Norman soldiers.

**Think about it**

13. Would it have been easy for the Saxons to attack the Normans in the White Tower?

Later, towers and curtain walls were built around the White Tower. The work was begun in 1194 A.D.

**Think about it**

14. Why do you think they are called curtain walls?

The towers and the curtain walls were planned by King Richard the Lionheart. By that time, the idea was to defend London from foreign invaders.

**Find out**

15. Has the fortress ever been attacked or captured?

The fortress has been used for many purposes since the time of William the Conqueror. The Kings and Queens of England lived there from time to time until about 1600 A.D. It was used as a royal arsenal, a royal mint, a royal menagerie.

**Find out**

16. What is an arsenal?
17. What happens at the royal mint?
18. What is a menagerie?

The Browns find the ancient fortress very interesting. Thousands of tourists visit the fortress every year. There are many things for them to see. Here are some of them. What are they?

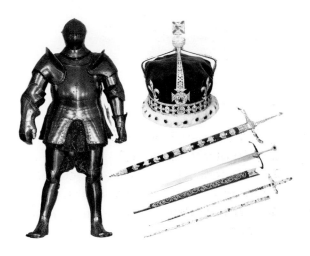

5

# Daydreams

Peter imagines he is back in the time of the Normans.

Look at the picture.

1. Is it raining in Peter's daydream?
2. Why might Mary be frightened?
3. What is Mr Brown doing?
4. How are the Norman soldiers dressed?
5. What are the houses of the Londoners like?
6. What makes you think they traded with foreign countries?
7. What weapons are used by the soldiers on the battlements?
8. Why would Peter's photograph be valuable if he could really take it?

Can you see the remains of a wall near the White Tower? That was built by the Romans centuries before.

Look at the picture.

7. Where does Peter imagine he is now?
8. Does the bowman have a good view from the top of the White Tower?
9. Where could people buy food in Saxon London?

You can see the Roman wall running right around London. Centuries before, the Romans built parts of London. They liked broad, straight streets.

Look at the picture.

10. What were the streets between the Saxon houses like?

The White Tower was built so that the Norman soldiers could watch everything.

It was easy to control a city from the top of a tower. From there the soldiers could see what was going on. A troop of soldiers could be sent to deal with any trouble.

**Think about it**

11. Where there times when the soldiers on the battlements could not see?

Can you see a church in the picture? St Paul's Cathedral was first built in 604 A.D. That building was burnt down in 1136 A.D.

**Find out**

12. What is on the site today?

The White Tower was very useful to the Normans. Except when it was dark or foggy, they could see what was happening in London. Even at those times, the Norman soldiers were safe. The White Tower was very difficult to attack.

**Before the next lesson**

Visit a travel agent's office. Collect brochures about the following countries – Belgium, Austria, Germany, Yugoslavia, Greece, the Greek Islands, Turkey, Cyprus and Israel.

# Getting there

Today, the Tower of London is a peaceful place. In the past it was, at times, dangerous. But this book is not about modern Britain. It is about a country called Israel.

1. Make a list of the Mediterranean countries marked on the map.
2. Why are they called Mediterranean countries?

**Think about it**

**3.** Why do many people go on holiday to the Mediterranean countries?

**Find out**

**4.** What kind of plane is this?
**5.** To what airline does it belong?

Look at the map.

This plane is leaving an airport in Britain

**6.** What is it called?

Can you see the route of the plane?

**7.** Over which countries does it fly?
**8.** What great range of mountains does it cross?
**9.** What islands can you see on the journey?
**10.** Where does it land?

It takes about four hours to fly by jumbo jet from Heathrow Airport to Ben Gurion Airport near Tel Aviv.

When people arrive in Israel, they find a very different country from Britain. There are palm trees growing in the streets and the climate is much warmer. Most of the year you need summer clothes in Israel.

**11.** What is our currency called?

**Find out**

**12.** What is the currency in Israel called?

Travellers from Britain to Israel change their money in the bank before going.

**13.** What nationality are you?

Two different races live in Israel.

**Find out**

**14.** What are they called?

Many people in Israel can speak several languages.

**Find out**

**15.** What language do Jewish people speak among themselves?
**16.** What language do the Arabs speak among themselves?

**Checking**

**17.** What two races were there in England at the time of William the Conqueror? (clue: p. 5)

Many of the Jews in Israel keep the laws of the Jewish religion.

**Find out**

**18.** What is the religion of many of the Arabs?

England has not been conquered since 1066 A.D. It is so long ago that the struggles between the Saxons and the Normans have been forgotten. But the State of Israel was set up in 1947 after many battles between the Jews and the Arabs. The situation is still tense today.

**Scrapbook**

Make a class scrapbook showing all the countries over which the jumbo jet flies on its way from Britain to Israel. (You will find the brochures you have collected useful.)

# Visit to the Old City

The Weissmans are a Jewish family living in Israel. They have a modern flat in Jerusalem.

**Checking**

**1.** What is the name of the airport near Tel Aviv? (clue: p. 8) Jerusalem is 61 kilometres from Tel Aviv.

Jerusalem is a modern city with shops and offices. But there are ancient parts.

**Checking**

**2.** What ancient part of London did the Browns visit? (clue: p. 4)

The ancient part of Jerusalem is called the Old City. Sometimes, the Weissmans visit the Old City.

Look at the picture.

**2.** How can you tell it is a hot day?
**3.** What is Mrs Weissman holding?

4. What is Mr Weissman doing?
5. How is Shimon helping?
6. How are Mrs Weissman and Rachel dressed?
7. Why do you think that the man carrying a camera has not been here before?
8. What would you call him?

Behind the Weissman family, you can see a famous wall. It is called the Western wall. Jewish men and women go there to pray.

9. Do the men and women pray together?

Compare the size of the stones with the size of the men.

10. What does that tell you about the Western wall?

Above the wall there is a beautiful building. It is called the Dome of the Rock.

11. What colour is the dome?

There are many colours on the rest of the building.

12. What is the main colour?

The Dome of the Rock is a famous mosque.

**Find out**

13. What is a mosque?

Mr Weissman is pointing at the steps which lead to the level of the Dome of the Rock. There is a group of guides, waiting to tell tourists about the mosque.

Look at the Jewish men who are praying at the Western wall.

14. Do the guides wear the same headgear as the Jewish men?

The guides are Arabs.

15. Why do Arabs rather than Jews show people the mosque?

Anyone visiting the Old City will see a great mixture of people. There will be Jews praying at the Western wall. There will be Arab guides waiting to show people the holy places of the religion of Islam. There will be many tourists who have come to Jerusalem to see the sights.

# Snapshots

## Checking

**1.** What Jewish holy place did the Weissmans see? (clue: p. 10)

**2.** To what religion does the Dome of the Rock belong? (clue: p. 11)

Do you remember Peter Brown?

**3.** What photograph did he take in his daydream? (clue: p. 6)

Let's pretend we can take snapshots of the holy places in Jerusalem as they were centuries ago.

Look at the picture.

**4.** Is the land level – or is it hilly?

Some people think that this hill became a holy place because men threshed corn here in ancient times. The grains of corn fell into a stone circle but the stalks were blown away in the wind.

**5.** What basic food is made from corn?

People in ancient times believed that bread was God's greatest gift to human beings.

This is how the place looked four thousand years ago.

The second picture shows the first Temple of the Jewish religion. It was built by the famous King Solomon. It was so long ago that it is difficult to give accurate dates. King Solomon probably died in 930 B.C.

**Think about it**

6. What do the letters A.D. and B.C. mean?
7. Which year came after 930 B.C. – 931 B.C. or 929 B.C.?

Solomon's Temple was destroyed by a Babylonian army in 586 B.C. The Jews were taken into captivity. They did not rebuild the Temple until peace came in 536 B.C. The Temple has had a stormy history.

The new Temple was not as grand as Solomon's Temple. But in about 20 B.C., King Herod the Great decided to build a much larger and much grander Temple than ever before. How much do you know about King Herod the Great?

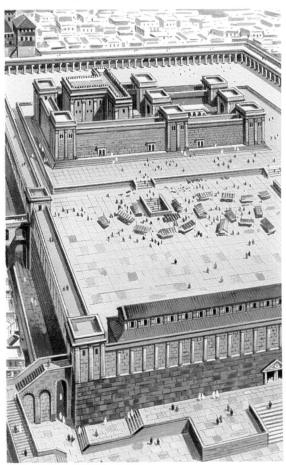

8. Who told him about Jesus' birth?

Look again at Solomon's Temple.

9. How many platforms were built on the hill?

King Herod decided to build the Temple on one huge platform. By the time it was finished, people could not see the top of the hill.

But King Herod's Temple was destroyed by the Romans in 70 A.D. The Temple has never been rebuilt.

This is a picture of the inside of the Dome of the Rock. Can you see the rock itself?

10. What did the men in ancient times do on this rock?

Muslims believe that the prophet Mohammed was carried up to heaven from this rock in 632 A.D. The rock became a holy place of the religion of Islam.

Because a mosque stands where the Temple used to stand, the Jews no longer go there to pray. But the Western wall is part of King Herod's Temple. It explains why the Jews pray there.

# More daydreams

When she sees the Western wall, Rachel daydreams about King Herod the Great.

Look at the picture.

1. Who does Rachel want Mrs Weissman to notice?
2. How is he carried about?
3. Can you guess what the man is showing him?

You can see how great a task King Herod gave his workmen.

4. What did he build on the sides of the hill?
5. What would the workmen use to make the foundations of the platform?

Look at the picture on page 12.

6. Was there a deep valley on this side of the hill?

Look at the picture below again.

7. What is Mr Weissman pointing out to Shimon?
8. Was the valley completely filled in?

Millions of tonnes of earth had to be brought to fill in the platform. Even more earth was brought to fill in the valley.

9. How was the earth brought?

Look at the picture on page 10.

**10.** Is part of Herod's bridge across the valley still to be seen today?

**Checking**

**11.** When did King Herod decide to start rebuilding the Temple? (clue: p. 13)

King Herod died in 4 B.C. But the work of rebuilding went on for many years after his death. It was not finished until about 63 A.D.

**Work it out**

**12.** About how long did the rebuilding of the Temple take?

**Checking**

**13.** When was the Temple destroyed by the Romans? (clue: p. 13)

**Work it out**

**14.** About how long did Herod's Temple last after it was finished?

King Herod the Great came from Idumea. He was not really a Jew. He was a friend of the Romans and ruled Israel by permission of the Roman Emperor, Augustus. The Jews did not like Herod.

**Checking**

**15.** Why did the Saxons dislike William the Conqueror? (clue: p. 5)

But Herod was the greatest builder in the history of Israel. He built palaces and fortresses. He even built whole towns. The grandest of his schemes was the rebuilding of the Temple.

Look at the picture again.

**16.** How do the men move the great blocks of stone?
**17.** What is used to pull them into position on the wall?

We can measure blocks of stone which were used in Herod's Temple. Some of them are six metres long and about a metre wide.

**Think about it**

**18.** What would we use today to get them into position?
**19.** What machinery do we use to move earth?
**20.** How do we carry earth long distances?

There were no cranes, bulldozers or lorries in Herod's time. Everything had to be done with ropes, tree trunks and carts.

# Testing

Here are two Time Charts
Copy them into your exercise book. Then
write down what happened at particular
dates. (A 'c' before a date means that we
cannot give it accurately.)

**Israel**

**B.C.**

2000 —

— 19th-18th century — first mention of
Jerusalem in Egyptian writings.

1000 — — c. 1010–970 – the reign of King David

— c. 930

— 587

— 537

— 37

— c. 20

— c. 6 – Jesus was born

— 4 – the death of King Herod the Great

0 —

**A.D.**

– c. 33 – Jesus died

– c. 63

– 70

– 632

1000 –

– 1190–1192 – the crusade in which
Richard the Lionheart took part

**Britain**

**B.C.**

– 55–54

0 –

**A.D.**

– 43 – the Roman conquest of Britain

– early fifth century – the Romans departed

– 604

1000 –

– 1066

– 1078

– 1136

# The Temple in Jesus' time

DAN ESCOTT

# Details

**Checking**

**1.** Why did William the Conqueror build the White Tower? (clue: p. 5)
**2.** How could London be controlled by a tower? (clue: p. 7)

This fortress was called the Antonia. It was built by King Herod the Great for exactly the same reason as William the Conqueror built the White Tower.

**Checking**

**3.** Why did the Saxons dislike William the Conqueror? (clue: p. 5)
**4.** Why did the Jews dislike King Herod the Great? (clue: p. 15)

The Jews disliked Herod as much as the Saxons disliked William. So Herod built the Antonia fortress to control the Temple platform. But this book is not about the time of Herod the Great. It is about the time of Jesus. When Jesus grew up, there was no king over Israel.

**Checking**

**5.** When did King Herod the Great die? (clue: p. 15)

We don't know when Jesus was born but we think it was probably 6 B.C.

**Think about it**

6. Why does that make our dating system wrong?

**Checking**

7. By whose permission did Herod rule Israel? (clue: p. 15)

When Jesus was grown up, Jerusalem was ruled by a Roman Governor.

8. Whose soldiers manned the Antonia fortress in Jesus' time?

Look at the picture on pages 18–19.

9. Where can you see soldiers?

**Find out**

10. What was the name of the Roman governor at the end of Jesus' life?

Look at the picture on pages 18–19.

11. Where are there men working?

**Checking**

12. About how long did it take to rebuild the Temple? (clue: p. 15)

This was one of the ways by which people could enter the Temple courts.

Jerusalem had its own special money.

13. Where can you see the tables of the money changers?

Can you see guards near the entrances?

14. How can you tell that they are guards?

There was a force of Temple police to keep people in order. They belonged to a special group of Jews called Levites. Their leader was called the Captain of the Temple.

Two different forces of men kept order at the Temple in Jesus' time. Roman auxiliary soldiers lived in the Antonia fortress and patrolled the covered way. In the Temple itself, a Jewish police force made sure that the rules were kept.

# More details

Look at the picture on pages 18–19.

You can see that most of the Temple platform was taken up with a huge court. A covered way ran around three sides.

**1.** What held up the covered way?

The large court was called the Court of the Gentiles.

**Find out**

**2.** What do Jews mean by the Gentiles?

The Court of the Gentiles was open to people of all nationalities.

**3.** What are these people selling in the Court of the Gentiles?

Look at the picture on pages 18–19.

Can you see smoke rising in front of the Temple building itself? Let's see what happened there.

At the Temple, Jews brought animals and birds for sacrifice.

**Find out**

**6.** What was a sacrifice?

The priests at the Temple killed birds and animals at the sacrifices.

Look at the picture.

**7.** What animal is about to be sacrificed here?

The blood of the animal was poured on to the fire in the altar.

There were all kinds of reasons for sacrifices. It could be done to give thanks to God. It could be done to ask God's forgiveness for wrongdoing.

Many of the men who brought animals for sacrifice bought them from the traders in the Court of the Gentiles.

When Jewish women went out in Jerusalem, they wore veils over their heads.

The inner courts of the Temple were for Jewish people only. Gentiles were forbidden to enter.

### Checking

**8.** What duties did some of the Levites carry out in the Temple? (clue: p. 21)

Look at the picture.

**9.** What duties, do you think, did these Levites carry out?

We know very little about the music they performed. But we have a great deal of the poetry which they sang.

### Find out

**10.** Which books of the Bible contain nothing but Hebrew poetry?
**11.** Are the poems still sung today?

The priests and the Levites were important people in the Temple. The Levites acted as Temple guards and some of them sang and played instruments at the services. The priests sacrificed animals and birds in front of the Temple building itself.

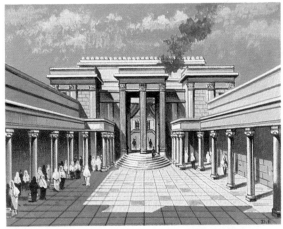

This was the Court of Women. It was really the Jewish family court, for men, women and children.

**12.** Who was there to stop Gentiles entering the inner courts?
**13.** Where does the gate at the end of the Court of Women lead to?
**14.** What could you see beyond the gate? (clue: p. 22)

# The Temple and its surroundings

In this picture, you can see the inner courts of the Temple.

This is from the other side so that you can see into the Temple itself.

Look at the picture on pages 18–19.

## Checking

**1.** What was the priest doing in front of the Temple? (clue: p. 22)
**2.** What did he do with the blood of the animal?

## Think about it

**3.** Who could enter the court around the Temple itself?

Around the sides of this court was the Court of the Men of Israel. No women or children were allowed to enter. Only the men could watch the sacrifices.

In the centre was the Court of the Priests. The sacrifices took place here.

Only the priests were allowed to enter the Temple itself.

**4.** What kind of man do you see at the entrance to the Temple building?

Every morning and evening, the priests on duty entered the Temple. They trimmed the wicks on the lamp. They offered incense to God.

## Find out

**5.** What is incense?
**6.** Is it used today?

Look at the picture again.

Can you see the table to the left of the small altar in the temple? That was the table of shewbread.

**7.** How many loaves were there on the table of shewbread?

## Find out

The people of Israel were divided into tribes.

**8.** How many tribes were there?

## Checking

**9.** What do people think happened on the Temple hill in ancient times? (clue: p. 12)

Bread was put in the Temple as a sign of God's goodness to his people.

## Checking

**10.** Who could enter the Court of the Gentiles?
**11.** Who could enter the Court of Women?
**12.** How near to the Temple itself could the men of Israel go?
**13.** What parts of the Temple were used only by the priests?

The Jews believed that God is in heaven. But they also believed that the Temple was his throne room.

## Find out

**14.** What is a throne room?

Look at the picture again.

Can you see a curtain hanging from the roof to floor inside the Temple? That was the veil of the Temple. Behind it was an empty room. It was the room of the presence of God.

Once a year, the High Priest went past the veil into the presence of God. The empty room was called the Holy of Holies.

## Find out

The high priest and other important people at the Temple had a council which governed affairs at the Temple.

**15.** What was it called?

# Testing

**Plans**

You are King Herod the Great's architect. The Antonia fortress is not yet built. What plans do you have to show him?

1. Make a ground plan.
2. Make an elevation plan (showing what the building will look like from one side).

Copy out the sentences and fill the spaces.

1. William the Conqueror built the White Tower to _____ London.
2. Herod the Great built the Antonia fortress to _____ the Temple.
3. _____ soldiers occupied the Antonia fortress when Jesus was grown up.
4. Anyone could enter the Court of the _____ at the Temple.
5. The Temple was first built by King _____ .
6. The _____ stands where the Temple stood in Jesus' day.
7. Today, Jewish men and women pray at the _____ of Herod's Temple.
8. A veil hung between the _____ and the rest of the Temple building.
9. The High Priest entered the holy of holies only _____ .
10. The Temple servants who sang in the choir were called _____.

**Choices**

Here are some questions and various answers. One answer is correct each time. Which one?

1. King Richard the Lionheart went on a crusade to the Holy Land in:
   a. 1092 A.D.
   b. 1109 B.C.
   c. 1190 A.D.

2. King Herod the Great's Temple was destroyed by:
   a. The Babylonians.
   b. The Romans.
   c. The prophet Mohammed.

3. William the Conqueror built the White Tower in:
   a. 1078 A.D.
   b. 1066 A.D.
   c. 1136 A.D.

4. Bread was put in the Temple:
   a. in case the priests were hungry.
   b. as a sign of God's goodness.
   c. as a gift to the High Priest.

5. There were money changers at the Temple because:
   a. The Temple had its own special money.
   b. they sold animals and birds for sacrifice.
   c. in case people needed change.

# The Old City of Jerusalem

# Visiting Jerusalem

**Checking**

1. Where do the Weissmans live? (clue: p. 10)
2. What part of Jerusalem did they visit?

Look at the picture on pages 28–29.

You can now see the whole of the Old City.

3. Where can you see the Temple platform?
4. How has the photographer taken this picture?

The Old City has always been a walled city.

**Checking**

5. What other ancient city have you seen with a wall around it? (clue: p. 7)

We are going to look around the Old City as it is today.

This is the church of the Holy Sepulchre.

**Find out**

6. What is a sepulchre?

Look at the picture. Then see if you can find the church on pages 28–29.

This deep valley is called the Valley of Kidron. Can you see the valley on pages 28–29.

**Checking**

Before King Herod the Great built the Temple platform, there was another deep valley.

7. What happened to it? (clue: p. 14)
8. Where was it?

Can you see this tower on pages 28–29.

**9.** Is it in the Old City?

The tower is the highest point in the surrounding countryside. It is on the Mount of Olives.

This is the Judean wilderness. Although trees and grass grow in Jerusalem, there is desert only a short distance away.

**10.** What is the wilderness like?

This is Mount Zion. People believe that the great King David was buried here.

**Checking**

**11.** When did he reign? (clue: p. 16)

David captured Jerusalem for the Israelites. He made Jerusalem a royal city.

**Checking**

**12.** Was Jerusalem there before David's time? (clue: p. 16)

The walls of the Old City of Jerusalem have been rebuilt many times in the last three thousand years. The builders have built them at different places at different times. In the next lesson, you will see the Old City as it was in Jesus' time.

# The Old City in Jesus' time

gardens outside the city

markets

NEW CITY

UPPER CITY

House of Caiaphas

LOWER CITY

# Plans

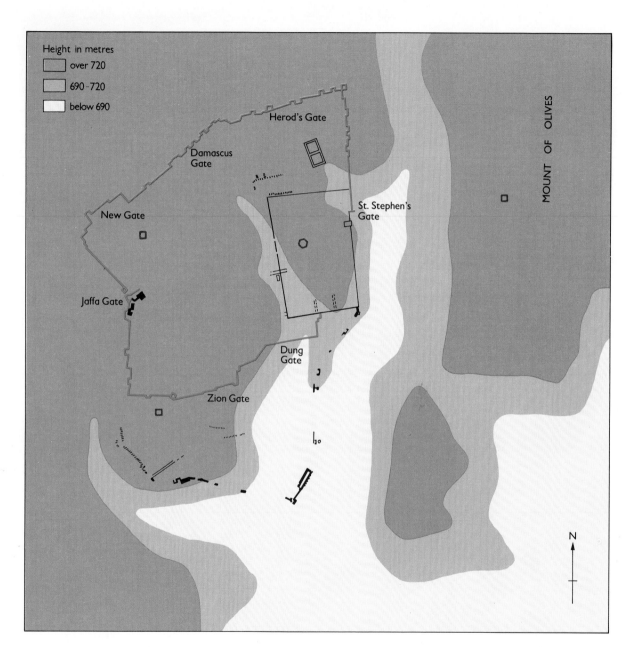

Copy this plan into your exercise book.

**1.** Is this the Old City as it is today or as it was in Jesus' time?
(clue: what is the shape of the building on the Temple platform?)

**2.** Label the following places on your plan:

**a.** the tower on the Mount of Olives
**b.** the church of the Holy Sepulchre
**c.** the Dome of the Rock
**d.** the Western Wall
**e.** the Valley of Kidron
**f.** Mount Zion

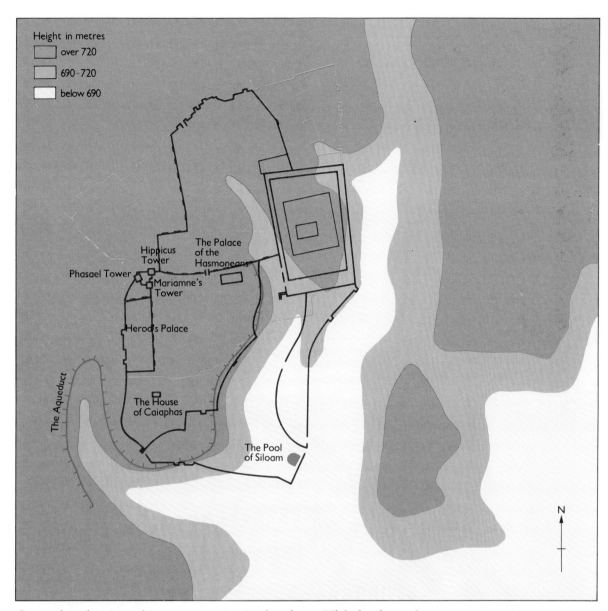

Height in metres
□ over 720
□ 690-720
□ below 690

Hippicus Tower
The Palace of the Hasmoneans
Phasael Tower
Mariamne's Tower
Herod's Palace
The Aqueduct
The House of Caiaphas
The Pool of Siloam

N

Copy the plan in red into your exercise book.

**3.** Is it the Old City as it is today or as it was in Jesus' time? (clue: p. 37)

**4.** Label the following places on your plan:
- **a.** the New City
- **b.** the Upper City
- **c.** the Lower City
- **d.** the Temple building

You can see that the Old City in Jesus' time had walls in different places from where they are today.

### Study the plans

**5.** Was the place where the Church of the Holy Sepulchre stands today inside or outside the walls in Jesus' time?

### Think about it

**6.** Why was there no church there in Jesus' time?

### Study the plans again

**7.** Is Mount Zion inside or outside the walls today?

**8.** Was it inside or outside the walls in Jesus' time?

The Old City covered a different area from the Old City today. The walls were in different places. Mount Zion was part of the city in Jesus' time but the site of the Church of the Holy Sepulchre was outside the city walls.

35

# The palace

Look at the picture on pages 32–33.

1. Where can you see this palace in the Jerusalem of Jesus' time?

Can you see it on the plan on page 35?

2. What was this palace called?
3. What were the names of the three towers near the palace?

We don't know for certain what this palace looked like. But we do have a description from someone who saw it. And we know it was built on a platform.

**Checking**

4. What else was built on a platform in Jerusalem? (clue: p. 14)

Herod the Great used exactly the same method for his own palace.

Look at the picture.

5. Were there curtain walls around Herod's palace?

Herod never felt safe in Jerusalem without soldiers and battlements. He was a king who mistrusted his own subjects.

But Herod was also worried about foreign invaders.

Look at the plan on page 35 again.

6. Were the three towers, Phasael, Hippicus and Mariamme near the city walls?

**Checking**

7. How were towers useful for keeping control of the surrounding countryside? (clue: p. 7)
8. Where else had Herod built a fortress to keep control of the surroundings? (clue: p. 20)

Look at the picture again.

9. What are people doing at the pool?
10. What might the servants be bringing to them?
11. What birds can you see in some of the courtyards?
12. Where could people watch a play or an entertainment?
13. Why do you think there is so much water around?

Although Herod's palace was defended like a fortress, life inside was very pleasant. There were plenty of servants to do the work. People could enjoy themselves with amusements of all kinds.

**Checking**

14. What fortress once had a menagerie? (clue: p. 5)

But King Herod had died in 4 B.C. When Jesus was grown up, Jerusalem was ruled by the Roman governor. When he was in Jerusalem, he lived in the palace of Herod the Great.

Look at the picture.

15. What kind of soldiers were manning the walls and the towers when Jesus was grown up?

Very little is left of the palace built by Herod. But we do have bits of plaster, showing the colours and designs on the walls of the palace.

16. Copy and colour one of the designs, making a whole wall of the pattern.

# Sightseeing

Imagine wandering around Jerusalem in Jesus' time. What would you see?

Look at the picture.

1. How did people get to the upper rooms and the rooftops?
2. How could they cross the street at roof level?

Many of the houses in ancient Israel were single storey. But in ancient Jerusalem, houses were often built higher.

3. What is the merchant in the picture doing?

In the Jewish religion, it was a duty to give to the poor.

4. What is the woman carrying?

5. Can you guess what the woman is going to do?

Look at the man begging. There were many poor people in ancient Jerusalem. There was not enough work for everyone.

Look at the picture on pages 32–33.

6. Where were there markets in the Jerusalem of Jesus' time?

Look at the picture on page 39.

7. Where did the wool come from?
8. What did the wool look like when it first arrived at the Wool Market?
9. How did the women make the wool thinner and looser?

Jerusalem was famous for its woollen garments. But turning a fleece into a garment is a complicated task. You can see some of the work being done.

Can you see women spinning the wool?

**Find out**

**10.** What is a spindle?

**11.** What is a distaff?

**12.** How did they work?

**13.** What took the place of a distaff and spindle centuries later?

Some of the work of turning a fleece into a garment is not shown in the picture. The wool had to be washed and bleached.

**14.** What happens when a material is bleached?

Some of the wool had to be dyed.

**15.** What happens when a material is dyed?

Look at the picture again.

**16.** How did the women make the threads of wool into cloth?

The making of woollen garments in ancient Jerusalem was always done by women.

**17.** What work did the men do in the Wool Market?

Some of the markets in ancient Jerusalem sold things which had been brought from elsewhere. Galilee, for instance, was famous for its linen.

**Find out**

**18.** From what plant is linen made?

To walk along a street or to visit a market in the Jerusalem of Jesus' time was very interesting. In other parts of the city, you could see builders, potters, vegetable merchants and bakers. Travelling merchants visited the city from many parts of the world.

# A rich man's house

Look at the picture on pages 32–33.

**1.** Was there a difference between the streets in the Upper City and the streets in the Lower City?

**Checking**

**2.** Who built broad, straight streets in ancient London? (clue: p. 7)
**3.** Where were there narrow, winding streets in ancient London?

**Think about it**

**4.** Are broad, straight streets planned or unplanned?
**5.** Are narrow, winding streets planned or unplanned?

**6.** Did the earliest people who lived in cities plan their streets – or did that come later?

The unplanned, winding streets of the Lower City show that is the oldest part of Jerusalem. That was Jerusalem when King David captured the city for the Israelites.

**Checking**

**7.** When did King David reign? (clue: p. 16)

Many rich people lived in Jerusalem in Jesus' time. Their houses were in the neat, planned streets of the Upper City.

**Checking**

**8.** What palace was in the Upper City? (clue: p. 37)

The picture on page 40 shows a rich man's house in Jerusalem at the time of Jesus. We don't know exactly what it looked like. But we know where it stood.

Look at the picture on pages 32–33.

**9.** Where can you see this house?

Look at the picture.

**10.** Does the house need fortifications like the Antonia?

**Checking**

**11.** Why did King Herod the Great need fortifications around his palace? (clue: p. 37)

In the country, Jewish houses were usually single-storey houses.

**Checking**

**14.** Were the houses in Jerusalem sometimes higher? (clue: p. 38)

Look at the picture.

**15.** How many storeys can you see in this house?

**Puzzle.** The archaeologists who have excavated this house have been surprised. There was a law among the Jews that they should not make pictures of anything.

But ordinary Jews, even if they were rich, did not need soldiers and defensive walls.

Look at the picture again.

**12.** What kind of a man can you see sitting at the gate?
**13.** Can you guess why he sat there?

These bits of plaster show that the law was broken in this house.

**16.** What can you see?

Nobody knows who lived in this house. But it has been called the House of Caiaphas.

**Find out**

**17.** Who was Caiaphas?

# The banquet

Rich people sometimes gave banquets.

The first task was to make a list of the guests.

Look at the picture.

**1.** Can you guess who is master of the house?

He is talking to his wife.

**2.** What is the servant girl bringing?

In the country, people drank wine out of stone-ware cups.

**Find out**

**3.** What is stone-ware?

Look at the picture again.

**4.** What did rich people in Jerusalem use?

**5.** What is the servant standing in front of his master doing?

The servant has a board covered on one side in wax. It is possible to write in the wax and then, afterwards, to smooth the wax out and write something else.

The master chooses his guests carefully. He lists them according to their importance. Where they will sit at the table will depend on how important they are.

Look at the picture again.

Do you see a man waiting to talk to the rich man? He is a skilled cook. Rich people employed special cooks for banquets. The cook was very well paid. But if the food did not please the guests, the cook had to pay money to each of them. The more important the guest, the more the cook had to pay.

The guests have been invited some time before the banquet. But they expect a servant to remind them on the day itself.

Look at the picture.

6. What meat are the guests going to eat?
7. What is being cooked in the other oven?

The ovens of Jesus' time contained hot charcoal.

**Find out**

8. What is charcoal?

A servant is boiling chickpeas.

**Find out**

9. What are chickpeas?

Look at the picture.

10. How are the guests being entertained?
11. Why are they clapping?
12. What are they drinking from?

The guests of honour sat on the right and on the left of the host at the banquet.

43

# Visitors

There were three great festivals at Jerusalem every year. There was Passover.

**Find out**

1. What did the Jewish people remember at Passover time?

There was Pentecost. The Jewish people gave thanks for the wheat harvest at Pentecost. There was Tabernacles.

**Find out**

2. What is a tabernacle?

Tabernacles was the time when the Jews gave thanks for the grape harvest.

3. What did they make out of the grapes?

Gathering the grapes was so great a task that people put up tents in the vineyards. It meant that they need not go home for the night.

Every Jew wanted to visit Jerusalem for the festivals. But many of the Jews lived abroad. Here is a map showing some of the places where Jews lived.

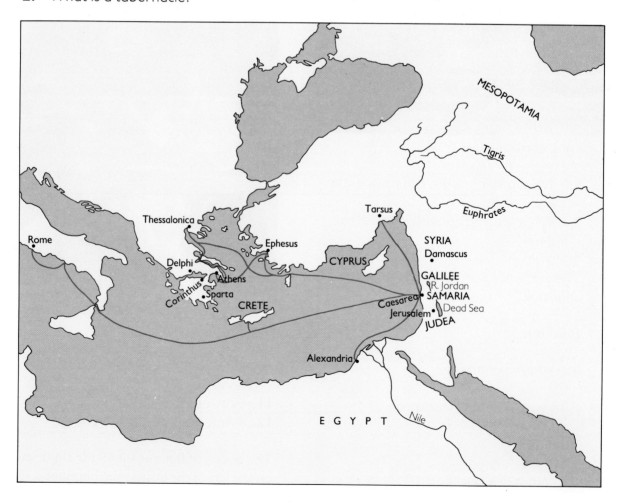

To visit Jerusalem meant travelling long distances.

Look at the map.

4. What port was there in Israel for people coming by sea?

Herod the Great built the port at Caesarea. You can still see part of his jetty under the water.

Look at the map again.

5. Which visitors could come by making a sea journey?
6. Which visitors were more likely to come by land?

There were inns at Jerusalem where visitors could stay. At least one synagogue had rooms for visitors.

But many pilgrims stayed outside the city. Or they stayed in villages not far from Jerusalem.

Look at the picture below.

7. Where are these visitors staying?
8. How have they carried their luggage?
9. Are they inside, or outside the city?
10. Where will they stay during the night?

Jerusalem was a busy place during festival times. Jews arrived from all over the world and many languages could be heard in the streets.

**Find out**

11. What language was usually spoken in Israel in Jesus' time?

**Checking**

12. What two languages are spoken in Israel today? (clue: p. 9)

Do you remember the banquet?

13. How were the guests at a banquet usually listed? (clue: p. 42)

At Passover time, rich people sent their servants into the city streets. They gathered up the beggars and poor people and invited them to a banquet.

# Think of a city

Let's take away all the changes which people have made to Jerusalem.

Look at the picture.

**1.** Does this seem a good site for a city?
**2.** It is a good site for a fortress?

### Checking

**3.** Which Israelite king captured Jerusalem and made it a royal city? (clue: p. 31)

The people who first lived here built a city because it was difficult to attack.

Look at the place where the Temple platform now stands.

### Checking

**4.** What did people in ancient times think about bread? (clue: p. 12)
**5.** Where were loaves of bread kept after the Temple had been built? (clue: p. 25)
**6.** What festival did the Jews hold to celebrate the wheat harvest? (clue: p. 44)

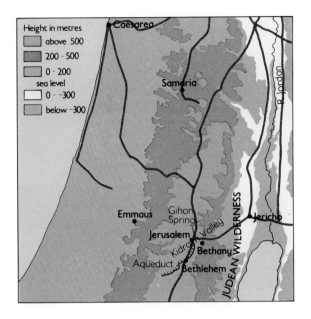

Here is a map of Jerusalem and its surroundings in Jesus' time.

You are going to make a journey from Jericho to Jerusalem. You walk with your donkey which is carrying food, water and a tent.

Look at the map.

**7.** What desert country are you going to cross?
**8.** What deep valley will you find on the way?

There was one other problem about making this journey. There were robbers on the road from Jericho to Jerusalem.

**Find out**

**9.** What story did Jesus tell about a man who was attacked by robbers on that road?

Look at the map again.

You are going to make a journey from Samaria to Jerusalem.

**10.** Does that seem difficult?

In Jesus' time, the Jews and the Samaritans were enemies. It was dangerous for a Jew to travel that way.

It was easier for Jews to travel to Jerusalem from the coast.

**Checking**

**11.** What port did Herod the Great build for travellers? (clue: p. 45)

But there were also gangs of robbers on that road. At least one village was called 'The village of robbers'.

Look at the map again.

The only natural water supply for Jerusalem is the Gihon spring.

**12.** Where is that?

A great deal less water comes from this spring in the summer than in the winter.

**Find out**

**13.** When does most of the rain fall in Jerusalem?

The people of Jesus' time had solved the problem.

**14.** What had they built to bring water to Jerusalem?
**15.** Where did the water come from?

Jerusalem was not a good place to build a city. It was difficult for travellers to get there. Water was a problem until the aqueducts were built. The soil around the city was poor and food had to be brought to the city. The place was a good site for a fortress but not for a city.

# Testing

Here are some everyday sights in modern Jerusalem.

1. Which of these, do you think, were exactly the same in Jesus' time?
2. Which of these, do you think, provided similar sights in Jesus' time?
3. One of these was definitely not to be seen in Jesus' time. Which?

The answers to the questions are upside down at the bottom of the page. Don't look until you have guessed.

**Wordsearch**

In the block of letters below, you will find ten words which have been used in the lessons.
Can you find them?

```
P X C B T F G X J B J G A N B
T H G H B C B R E A D C N S N
T C A I A P H A S N J T T C K
P A S S O V E R H Q B W O O L
F B N V A L T A R U Z P N B W
C B S C A E S A R E A V I Z L
X Z T E M P L E V T C S A A B
```

When you have found the ten words, write them down. Then explain what they mean.

**Time Chart**

Put these people in the order in which they lived:

Richard the Lionheart, Jesus, Herod the Great, King David, William the Conqueror, King Solomon

1. The basket and the donkey
2. The beggar, the money changer's shop and the guard on the Temple platform
3. The kitchen tap

49

# How do we learn?

Look at the picture

**1.** What is this baby boy doing?

**Think about it**

**2.** Did the baby do this when he was first born?

When babies are born, they need to learn everything. One of the first things they learn is how to recognise their mothers.

**3.** How does this baby show that he recognises his mother?

**Find out**

**4.** At what age does a baby usually start talking?

In the first few years of our lives, we learn faster than at any other time.

**Think about it**

**5.** What language does an English baby learn?
**6.** What language does a Jewish baby in Israel learn?

Later in our lives we need to be taught.

**7.** What is happening here?

People sometimes say that the three Rs need to be taught first.

**Find out**

**8.** What are the three Rs?
**9.** Do they really all begin with R?

**Find out**

**10.** Why is learning to read Hebrew different from learning to read English?

50

As we get older, we learn more and more complicated ideas.

Look at the picture.

**11.** Why does the car have a letter 'L' on it?

Driving a car is quite complicated. There are many rules.

### Find out

**12.** What is the book of rules in Britain called?
**13.** What basic driving rule is different in America or France?

People learn in a great many different ways. Small babies learn from their mothers. Schoolchildren learn from their teachers. But learning never stops. There is always something new to learn.

### Think about it

**14.** Both these men live in Israel, but have they learnt different things?

Jesus was a teacher of religion. But he did not teach in a classroom. Everywhere he went, people came to listen to him.

### Think about it

**15.** What do teachers of religion talk about?
**16.** Has anyone ever seen God?

### Checking

**17.** What did the Jews have in the Temple for the presence of God? (clue: p. 25)

Jesus' method was to teach about God, who has never been seen, by talking about the things which people *have* seen.

### Think about it

**18.** Would Jesus talk about country life if he was talking to the shopkeeper?
**19.** Would he talk about town life if he was talking to the shepherd?

# Training the disciples

Jesus spent most of his life in Galilee. But he visited Jerusalem many times for the festivals.

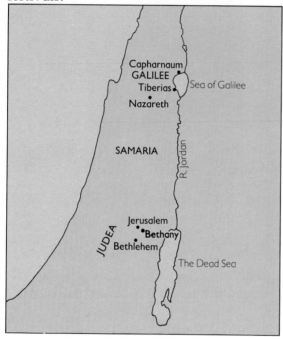

Look at the map.

1. In what part of Irsael was Jerusalem?
2. What part of the country lay between Galilee and Judea?

Galilee was a fertile part of Israel with many small towns and villages.

Look at the picture.

3. Is Jesus in Jerusalem – or in Galilee?
4. What is the lake in the picture called?

**Think about it**

5. Did Jesus talk about town life, or country life, when he was in Galilee?

Wherever Jesus went, he was followed by large crowds. But he also taught his disciples. They became his disciples when he was in Galilee.

**Find out**

6. What does the word 'disciple' mean?

Look at the picture

7. How many disciples were there?

**Checking**

8. Where have you seen this bird before? (clue: p. 4)

52

'Look at Brother Raven,' said Jesus. 'Does he sow? Does he plough? Does he harvest?'

**9.** Why could a raven not do such things?
**10.** Why would a raven not do such things?

**Think about it**

**11.** What occupation is Jesus talking about?
**12.** Is it a town occupation – or a country occupation?
**13.** What trades might he have talked about if they had lived in Jerusalem? (clue: p. 51)

'Look at Sister Iris,' said Jesus. 'Does she weave? Does she make fine clothes?'

**Checking**

**14.** What cloth was made in Jerusalem? (clue: p. 38)
**15.** What cloth was made in Galilee?

Look at the picture.

**16.** Why does the iris not need to do such things?

By pointing at a raven and an iris, Jesus taught his disciples that they were not to do ordinary jobs like other people. They were to spend their time learning from him. One day, they too would be teachers of religion.

**Think about it**

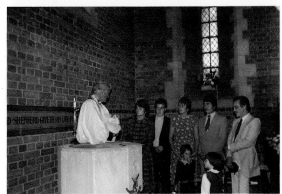

**17.** What are these people doing?
**18.** Do they have ordinary jobs as well?

The work which Jesus began with his disciples is still going on today.

# The men who followed Jesus

We know quite a lot about some of Jesus' disciples. Others we only know by name.

Peter was the most forceful character. Do you remember the famous story of how Peter became a disciple?

Look at the picture.

## Find out

1. How long had the fishermen been fishing before Jesus came?
2. What had they caught?
3. What happened when Jesus went fishing with them?
4. Who is in the other boat?
5. What is his brother Andrew doing?

Peter and Andrew both became disciples after the great catch of fish. Jesus said they would become fishers of men.

## Think about it

6. What do you think that meant?

Two of the disciples had Greek Names – Andrew and Philip.

Here is a picture of another famous story about Jesus. There are about five thousand people in the crowd. They are far away from the shops. 'How are we going to feed these people?' asked Jesus.

Look at the picture.

7. What has the boy got in his basket?
8. Who has brought him to Jesus?
9. What is Philip doing?

'Two hundred denarii's worth of food would not feed them,' said Philip.

A denarius was a Roman coin used in Jesus' time.

It was reckoned to be the amount of money a man could earn in a day.

**Think about it**

**10.** Can you decide how much two hundred denarii would be worth today?

**Find out**

**11.** What happened in the story?

Matthew also became a disciple.

**12.** Why would people have said that he was a most unlikely person to become a disciple?

Look at the picture.

**13.** Which disciple do you not recognise?

His name was Judas Iscariot.

**14.** What is he carrying?

Judas Iscariot looked after the money for Jesus and the rest of the disciples.

In this lesson, we have seen five of Jesus' disciples.

**15.** Make a list of them.

We will learn about three others – James, John and Thomas – later in this book. But we know practically nothing of James the son of Alphaeus, Simon the Zealot, Bartholomew and the other Judas.

# Jesus' teachings

## Checking

**1.** How did Jesus teach about God? (clue: p. 51)

**2.** Why did he talk about the raven and the iris when he was in Galilee?

Look at the picture.

**3.** What are Jesus and the disciples watching?

**4.** Which hand does the ploughman use to control his plough?

**5.** What does he have in the other hand?

**6.** What is it for?

**7.** How does the plough work?

Can you see a stick where the furrow will end?

**8.** Why does the ploughman look at the stick as he ploughs?

## Think about it

**9.** What would be likely to happen if the ploughman looked over his shoulder?

**Try it yourself**

Put two dots some distance apart on a piece of paper. Try drawing a straight line between them. Can you do it? Now try again while looking over your shoulder.

'That ploughman knows,' said Jesus, 'that his furrow will only be straight if he keeps his eye on the stick.'

**Think about it**

10. Why does the ploughman want a straight furrow?

The ploughman is doing many things.

11. Make a list of them.

'People do many things in life,' said Jesus. 'But God is more important than anything else. People must concentrate on God just as the ploughman concentrates on the stick.'

**Checking**

12. Why did Jesus say that his disciples should not do ordinary jobs? (clue: p. 53)

Jesus' teachings are not easy to follow.

Look at the picture.

13. What is this footballer about to do?
14. Is he concentrating on God – or on the ball?

**Think about it**

15. Who would Jesus say has given the footballer life?
16. Who would he say has given him the ability to score the goal?

In Jesus' teaching, a man cannot do anything without the gifts that God has given him. But it is easy to forget when you are playing a game of football.

**Think about it**

17. Was the ploughman doing many things at once?
18. On what did he concentrate while he did them?
19. Is it possible to remember God while you are doing something else?

Jesus wanted people to remember God whatever they were doing.

**Checking**

20. What happened to the ploughman when he looked over his shoulder?

'If the ploughman wants to keep his furrow straight,' said Jesus, 'he must concentrate on the stick. And if you want to keep your lives straight, you must concentrate on God.'

# Teaching in Jerusalem

## Checking

1. In which part of Israel did Jesus spend most of his life? (clue: p. 52)

Towards the end of his life, Jesus moved to Jerusalem. His disciples went with him. Sometimes they stayed in the city. Sometimes they stayed in the towns and villages of Judea.

## Checking

2. In which part of Israel was Jerusalem? (clue: p. 52)

Look at the picture below.

3. Where is Jesus teaching this crowd? (clue: pp. 18–19)
4. In which court is he standing? (clue: p. 22)
5. What kinds of people could not enter the inner courts?
6. Who were there to stop them?

Some of the important religious leaders of the time were called Pharisees. They studied the laws of the Jewish religion. They applied the laws to everyday life. But some of them thought only the laws mattered.

'Imagine,' said Jesus, 'two men coming to the Temple to pray.'

Look at the picture.

The man at the top of the steps is the Pharisee in Jesus' story.

**7.** What can you see on the pavement near the kneeling man?
**8.** Can you guess his occupation?
**9.** Did the people of Israel like such people?
**10.** In which court is he kneeling?

Jesus then told the people what prayers the two men said.

**The Pharisee's prayer**

'I thank God that I am not like other men. I am not greedy. I am not dishonest. I give a great deal of money to the poor. I go without food two days a week. I am glad I am not like that tax collector down there.'

In his prayer, the Pharisee mentions how he obeys the laws of the Jewish religion.

**Checking**

**11.** What did the laws say about the poor? (clue: p. 38)

**Find out**

**12.** Where can you find the law which says that it is wrong to steal?

**Think about it**

**13.** What other two laws did the Pharisee say he kept?
**14.** Was the Pharisee concentrating on God – or on his understanding of the laws?
**15.** Was he praying – or was he boasting?

**The tax collector's prayer**

'Please God, have mercy on me, sinner that I am.'

**Think about it**

**16.** Could the tax collector be proud of the laws that he kept?
**17.** Was the tax collector really praying?

**Find out**

**18.** In what ways did many tax collectors do wrong?

'One of these men,' said Jesus, 'was forgiven for the things he had done wrong.'

**Think about it**

**19.** Can you decide which man was forgiven?
**20.** Is anyone perfect?

Jesus did not teach that the laws of the Jewish religion were wrong. But he did teach that keeping the laws was not enough. Because he concentrated on the laws instead of concentrating on God, the Pharisee had turned his prayer into a boast. But nobody is perfect. Like the tax collector, everyone must trust in God's mercy.

# God's banquet

### Checking

1. Where was Jesus when he talked about the raven and the iris? (clue: p. 53)
2. Where was Jesus when he talked about the two men going to the Temple to pray? (clue: p. 58)

5. In what part of the city could such houses be found? (clue: p. 40)
6. What is Jesus doing?

'A rich man decided to give a banquet,' said Jesus to the crowd.

Look at the picture.

3. What kind of a house can you see in the background? (clue: p. 40)

### Checking

4. Were such houses in Galilee – or in Jerusalem?

### Checking

7. What was the rich man's first task? (clue: p. 42)
8. In what order did he put the guests?
9. What skilled person did he employ?
10. When were the guests first invited?
11. When did they receive a second invitation?

### Think about it

You are invited to the rich man's banquet. But you cannot attend. You are getting married that day.

**12.** Is that a reasonable excuse for not attending?
**13.** Do you send your apologies after the first invitation – or do you wait until the messenger comes on the day of the banquet?
**14.** What would you say about people who did not bother to reply until the messenger came?

'When the messenger went out on the day of the banquet,' said Jesus, 'he told the guests that everything was ready. The food was cooked and the table had been laid. But every single guest refused to come. They all made excuses.'

**15.** What do you think of those guests?

Look at the picture.

**16.** Where does the messenger find this guest?

### Think about it

**17.** Could the ploughing have been put off to another day?

All the guests made similar excuses.

'When the rich man heard,' said Jesus, 'he was very angry. He sent his servants into the streets of the city. They brought in the poor people, the cripples, the blind people and the beggars. They enjoyed the rich man's banquet.'

### Checking

**18.** When did rich men in Jerusalem usually give a banquet to the poor? (clue: p. 45)

'When you come to know God,' said Jesus, 'it is like being invited to a banquet. I am God's messenger. I have come with God's invitation.'

### Think about it

**19.** What do you think Jesus meant when he said that knowing God was like being invited to a banquet?

Jesus taught that knowing God greatly enriches the lives of human beings. A person who comes to know God is like a beggar being invited to a banquet.

### Checking

**20.** Did the Pharisee in Jesus' story know God – or did he think only of the laws? (clue: p. 59)

Nobody who really knows God can boast in his presence.

# Surprises for a rich man

Look at the picture.

1. Who is coming to speak to Jesus?
2. Who are the people who are following him?
3. What kind of man is sitting at the gate to the house?

'Tell me, master,' said the rich man, 'how can I please God?' 'Don't ask me,' said Jesus, 'because you know already.'

**Find out**

4. Where could the laws of the Jewish religion be found?

'What do I know?' asked the rich man. 'That you must not steal, murder or tell lies,' said Jesus. 'And you must love other people as much as you love yourself.' 'I do my best,' said the rich man, 'but where do I fail?'

**Think about it**

5. What did the rich man own?
6. Did other people own such things?

'Start off,' said Jesus, 'by selling that house. You can give the money to the poor.'

**Checking**

Do you remember the guests who rudely refused to come to a banquet?

7. What was the guest doing when he should have been going to the banquet? (clue: p. 61)
8. What interested him most – the banquet or the ploughing?

Look at the picture.

**9.** What is the rich man doing?

**Think about it**

**10.** Do you think the rich man would really sell his house and give the money to the poor?

'Rich people,' said Jesus, 'would like to accept God's invitation. But they are really more interested in other things. That rich man thinks more of his house than he does of God.'

Look at the picture at the bottom of the page.

**11.** What is Jesus holding up in his hand?

'Can you push a camel through the hole in this needle?' asked Jesus.

**Think about it**

**12.** Why did the people in the crowd laugh?

'It is easier to push a camel through this hole,' said Jesus, 'than to get a rich man to accept God's invitation.'

**Think about it**

**13.** Was Jesus' story about the Pharisee and the tax collector likely to anger the Pharisees?
**14.** Was Jesus' advice to the rich man likely to anger the rich people of Jerusalem?

Jesus was not afraid to anger rich and important people. He wanted people to concentrate on God rather than on other things – even on the laws of the Jewish religion.

**Think about it**

You are given a present by your friend.

**15.** Which is the more important – your friend or the present?
**16.** Who would Jesus say had given the laws to the Jewish people?
**17.** Which was the most important – the laws or the giver of the laws?
**18.** Was it Jesus' purpose to anger people like the Pharisees – or was his purpose to point out that they should concentrate on God?

Jesus was not attacking the Jewish religion in his teachings. But he was attacking the way some people treated the religion. He was not attacking riches either, but only the way in which people treated their riches.

63

# Lazarus

Look at the picture.

**1.** Who is Jesus talking about now?
**2.** What would we call this man?

**Checking**

**3.** Are there still such people in Jerusalem today? (clue: p. 48)
**4.** What can you see on his face and on his hands?
**5.** What is the dog doing?

Many wild dogs roamed the streets of Jerusalem.

**6.** Does the beggar try to get rid of the dog?

**Checking**

**7.** What did the Jewish religion say about the poor? (clue: p. 38)

'Look at poor Lazarus over there,' said Jesus. 'The guests at the rich man's house throw the food they don't want under the table. When the servants sweep up, they give the food to Lazarus. It just about keeps him alive.'

**Checking**

**8.** What did the rich man say about his own behaviour? (clue: p. 62)

'There is a famous story,' said Jesus. 'It can explain what I think about the rich man.'

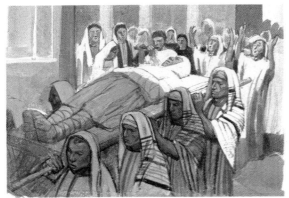

Look at the picture.

**9.** What has happened to the rich man?
**10.** Why are there so many people?

Look at the picture.

**11.** What has happened to Lazarus?
**12.** Does he have mourners?
**13.** What creatures follow Lazarus to his burial?

Look at the picture.

**14.** What has happened to Lazarus in the land of the dead?

**Checking**

**15.** Where did guests of honour sit at a banquet? (clue: p. 43)

The host at this banquet is Abraham, father of the Jewish nation.

Look at the picture again.

**16.** What has happened to the rich man?

'Please, Father Abraham,' says the rich man, 'send Lazarus to bring me some water.'

**17.** Why does the rich man want water?

'In your lifetime,' says Abraham, 'you had your good things and Lazarus had evil things. Now you suffer just as he suffered then. You could have helped him, but he cannot help you. There is a great space between us which he cannot cross.'

**Think about it**

**18.** Had the rich man and Lazarus really died – or only in Jesus' story?
**19.** What should the rich man do before it is too late?

Jesus wanted people to change their lives right away. The time would come when it would be too late.

**Checking**

**20.** What was Jesus' advice to the rich man? (clue: p. 62)

# The little flock

The longer Jesus stayed in Jerusalem, the more enemies he made.

## Checking

1. What did he say which angered many of the Pharisees? (clue: p. 63)
2. What did he say which angered many rich people?

Jerusalem was the holy city. But many of the people who lived there were more interested in other things than they were in God. This was true even in the Temple itself.

## Checking

3. Who were the people who looked after these stalls? (clue: p. 21)
4. Where did they carry out their business?

When they changed the money of the visitors to Jerusalem, they did not give the full value. It was a way of making money for themselves.

## Think about it

5. Do you think they were more interested in the money – or in God?

**Find out**

**6.** What did Jesus do to the tables of the money changers?

**Checking**

**7.** Why were these people selling animals and birds? (clue: p. 22)
**8.** Where did they carry out their business?

Even the people who sold animals and birds for the sacrifices at the Temple were there to make money. Jesus knocked over their seats.

**Find out**

**9.** What did Jesus say when he did so?

There were many evils in the holy city. As time went by, Jerusalem became a dangerous place for Jesus and his disciples. Because of his teachings, many important people wanted Jesus killed. It was frightening for the disciples.

'This shepherd,' said Jesus, 'knows every sheep by name.'

**Find out**

**10.** What famous Hebrew poem compares God with a shepherd?

Look at the picture.

**11.** Is there a danger to the flock of sheep?
**12.** Who will protect the sheep?

'God is like the shepherd,' said Jesus. 'He knows you and will care for you.'

Look at the picture.

**13.** What has happened to the shepherd's flock?
**14.** For which animal is this flock dangerous?

'But this world is a dangerous place for the people who follow me,' said Jesus. 'I am sending you out like lambs among wolves.'

**Think about it**

**15.** Is a lamb a dangerous animal?
**16.** Why did Jesus compare his followers with lambs?

Jesus knew that his teachings would anger many people. But he and his disciples were not to be afraid. They were to be harmless men in a dangerous world. Jesus sometimes called his followers his little flock.

# Disciples and friends

Apart from the disciples, Jesus had many other followers. Some of them were women. The most famous was Mary Magdalene.

Look at the picture.

**I.** Are they in Jerusalem – or in Galilee?

Mary came from Magdala, a town near the Sea of Galilee. The Bible says that before she met Jesus she had seven evil spirits. Nobody knows what that means.

**2.** What do you think it means?

Look at the picture.

These sisters were followers of Jesus. They lived in Bethany, a small village outside Jerusalem. Can you find Bethany on the map on page 52? The names of the sisters were Martha and Mary. Martha is sweeping the house.

**3.** What is Mary doing?

When this happened, it led to a quarrel between the two women.

**4.** What would you say if your sister sat around while you were working?
**5.** Why did Jesus say that Mary was doing more important work than Martha?

## Checking

**6.** What kind of work were Jesus' disciples to do? (clue: p. 53)

Salome was a follower of Jesus. Her two sons, James and John, were disciples.

## Find out

**7.** When did they become disciples?

John is carrying a scroll.

'You have compared God's message with an invitation to a banquet,' said Salome. 'Can my two sons be the guests of honour?'

## Checking

**8.** Where did the guests of honour sit at a banquet? (clue: p. 43)

## Think about it

**9.** Do you think the question annoyed the other disciples?
**10.** Do you think it was right for Salome to ask such a question?

'God will decide such things,' said Jesus. 'It is not something I can promise.'

We do hear of other followers of Jesus but we know nothing about them. There was Joanna, and Mary the mother of James.

## Checking

**11.** How many disciples did we see in the lesson about 'The men who followed Jesus'? (clue: pp. 54–55)

## Think about it

**12.** What two disciples have you see in this lesson?
**13.** Were any of the disciples women?

Women were treated differently from men in Jesus' time.

## Checking

**14.** Were there parts of the Temple which they could not enter? (clue: p. 25)

But in the Jewish religion, they were treated with respect. And Jesus taught women as well as men about God and the gifts that God gives.

# Testing

Jesus was always thinking of new ways of describing the disciples.

Look at the pictures.

1. Which of these creatures is dangerous?
2. Which is harmless?
3. Which has the reputation of being very cunning?

**Think about it**

Copy the sentences and fill in the spaces. 'You must be as cunning as a _____ ,' said Jesus, 'and as harmless as a _____ '.

A wedding was always followed by a great banquet.

4. What do we call a wedding banquet?
5. What kind of clothes do people wear at a wedding?

Look at the picture.

6. Where can you see the bride and the groom?
7. What is unusual about one of the guests?

Nobody could ever be quite certain when a wedding feast was going to begin in Jesus' time. The bridegroom and his friend made a procession to the home of the bride. They coaxed her to come to the wedding banquet. Sometimes it took a long time.

**Think about it**

8. How could people be sure of being properly dressed for the wedding banquet?

At the wedding banquet in the picture, the bridegroom has brought the bride much earlier than expected.

**Think about it**

**9.** Why is one of the guests still dressed in old clothes?

'The coming of God,' said Jesus, 'is like the coming of a bride and bridegroom to a wedding. You never know when it is going to happen.'

**10.** What is the meaning of Jesus' story?

**Checking**

**11.** What food was served at the banquet we saw being prepared?

Copy out the sentences and fill in the spaces.

**12.** The tax collector at the Temple prayed but the Pharisee _____ .
**13.** The guests invited to the banquet rudely _____ to come.
**14.** The rich man invited the _____ instead.
**15.** Jesus told the rich man to start by _____ .
**16.** Jesus said that it was easier to push a _____ through the eye of a needle than to get a _____ to accept God's invitation.
**17.** In Jesus' story, Lazarus was _____ at a banquet given by Abraham.
**18.** The ploughman kept his eye on the _____ at the end of the _____ .

**Ending 1**

# The journey

Look at the picture.

**1.** Where are Jesus and his disciples?

Look at the picture on pages 28–29.

**2.** Is there scenery like this near Jerusalem?

Look at the map on page 52.

**3.** What is the stretch of water you can see in the picture?
**4.** What are Jesus and his disciples doing?
**5.** How do you know that they have stayed there some time?

From time to time, Jesus went somewhere quiet to pray. He taught his disciples to do the same thing.

**Find out**

**6.** When did Jesus spent forty days in the Judean wilderness?

The disciples and Jesus stayed in the wilderness for some time. But it was nearly time for the Passover.

**Checking**

**7.** What did every Jew want to do at festival time? (clue: p. 44)
**8.** Where did people stay in and around Jerusalem? (clue: p. 45)

Jesus decided that he would return to Jerusalem for the passover.

Look at the picture.

**9.** What is the disciple called Thomas doing?

Thomas is the one disciple we know about who has not been described in this book.

### Checking

**10.** What were the names of the other disciples? (clue: pp. 54–55)

### Think about it

When people are frightened, they either get angry or they want to run away.

**11.** How is Thomas behaving?
**12.** Why should he be frightened? (clue: p. 67)

Look at the picture.

**13.** Did Thomas persuade Jesus not to go to Jerusalem?

### Checking

**14.** What kinds of people had Jesus' teachings angered? (clue: p. 80)

Jesus may have angered important people. But the ordinary people loved to hear his teachings.

Look at the picture again.

**15.** From where are some of the people coming to meet Jesus?

### Checking

**16.** Why were there travellers on the road at that time? (clue: p. 45)

In the picture, Jesus and his disciples are on the Mount of Olives.

**17.** What deep valley lies between the Mount of Olives and Jerusalem? (clue: pp. 32–33)

### Think about it

**16.** What is often laid out nowadays when an important visitor is coming?

Look at the picture.

**17.** What are the people doing here?

Just as we lay out a red carpet when a special visitor arrives, so the people of Jesus' time laid branches and spread their cloaks in front of him. It was like the coming of a great king.

**Ending 2**

# The dangerous festival

## Checking

1. Which of Jesus' disciples was most worried by his coming to Jerusalem? (clue: p. 73)
2. Who governed Jerusalem at the time? (clue: p. 37)
3. Where did he live?

## Find out

4. What was his name?

Passover time was also worrying for the Roman governor and his soldiers.

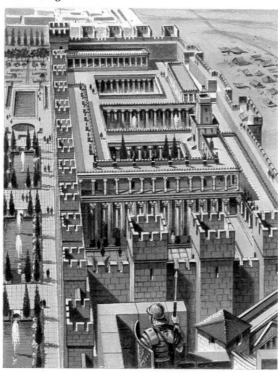

## Checking

5. What were the names of the three towers near Herod's Palace? (clue: p. 37)

This Roman auxiliary soldier is standing at the top of Mariamme.

Look at the plan on page 35.

6. In which direction is the soldier looking?
7. What would he see if he looked to his left?
8. What would he see if he looked behind him?
9. What would be happening in the streets at Passover?

Look at the picture.

10. Is the palace itself very crowded?
11. Why have people put up tents outside the city wall? (clue: p. 45)

## Checking

12. What other fortresses did the Roman soldiers occupy? (clue: p. 20)

The Roman governor and his soldiers found the festivals worrying because there were so many people crowded into the city. Many of the Jews would have liked to raise an army to throw out the Romans. But the Romans did not have a large garrison at Jerusalem.

Look at the map on page 8. Their nearest army was in Syria to the north.

That particular festival was worrying, too, for the Sanhedrin.

## Find out

13. What was the Sanhedrin? (clue: p. 30)